Music for French Horn & Piano

BEGINNING FRENCH HORN SOLOS
Volume 2

Myron Bloom: *French Horn*
Harriet Wingreen: *Piano*

ISBN 978-1-59615-211-3

Music Minus One

EXCLUSIVELY DISTRIBUTED BY

HAL•LEONARD®

Visit Hal Leonard Online at
www.halleonard.com

Contact us:
Hal Leonard
7777 West Bluemound Road
Milwaukee, WI 53213
Email: info@halleonard.com

In Europe, contact:
Hal Leonard Europe Limited
42 Wigmore Street
Marylebone, London, W1U 2RN
Email: info@halleonardeurope.com

In Australia, contact:
Hal Leonard Australia Pty. Ltd.
4 Lentara Court
Cheltenham, Victoria, 3192 Australia
Email: info@halleonard.com.au

PERFORMANCE GUIDE
COMMENTARY BY MYRON BLOOM

BACH
Chorale Prelude — Herzlich tut mich verlangen

In this Chorale Prelude, we again have a piece which was not written for the horn. And yet, if we apply the knowledge which is necessary to bring out the true quality, the horn can sound most lovely. Bach was a very religious composer. It is that kind of feeling that we must recognize when playing this piece.

The quarter notes in the opening bar must be as legato as possible, articulated with no space between the notes. To get this, there must be an enormous control of the air.

I would suggest playing this with a metronome so that the sixteenth notes and the dotted eighths are exactly in their place. If ever anyone wrote with a musical line, it was Bach. And this has to be brought out from the opening bar to the very end . . . one glorious musical line.

BALLATORE
Serenata

Playing legato is the main problem in Pietro Ballatore's Serenata. Notice the eighth note rest in measure 6. You must not lose your breath support on this rest. There must be an accent of expression on the downbeat quarter note, and then the eighth note must not die away. You will need an unremitting column of air.

BEETHOVEN
Little Rondo

It is important to keep the musical line moving forward in this Little Rondo. This is done by breath control. The air must never stop its forward motion. When you ride a bicycle up and down hill, you don't at any time lose the forward motion of the pedal. This analogy is appropriate to horn playing. Just remember, when you make a crescendo towards a louder dynamic, the air column must open up. It must get wider. Diaphragm support that impels the air column must always remain constant.

SCHUBERT
Andantino

This is one of the most sublime, and at the same time, simplest melodies ever written. The key to playing it well is to be artless. Let the rhythm, shape of phrase, and harmony unite to make this music as warm and expressive as possible. The air column must be as constant as possible, especially at the ends of phrases. Do not let them die, but keep the breath moving until the very last whisper of the note.

R. STRAUSS
Allerseelen

This is a transcription of one of Richard Strauss' most popular songs. To play it well, you must handle the horn as vocally as possible. The repeated eighth notes in the beginning should be articulated with a "da," so that they are very legato, with no separation. Legato is of the utmost importance in playing a piece like this. You will need to take a quick gulp of air before the *fortissimo* in measure 33.

TCHAIKOVSKY
Kamarinskaya

This is a lovely piece which offers several styles of articulation. It is important to get as much resonance in the staccato as possible, so that it does not become dry. The sound must stop between each eighth note, and in spite of this, you must preserve the musical line. The staccato passages occur both in *piano* and *forte* dynamics. Except for the volume of sound, they should be played in the same way. The articulation should not change with the dynamic level. The legato, which begins in measure 13, should be as smooth as possible, to provide contrast. The staccato should be articulated with the syllable, "ta." (Use the syllable "da" for the legato.) There must be no doubt that this is happening. It must be very definite.

KAPLAN
Soliloquy

In the Soliloquy by David Kaplan, you again have a basic legato articulation, which should never stop the flow of the line. Even in measures 8 and 9, where there is a little separation between the quarter note and the half note, the line must continue to move forward without any hint of dryness. You cannot spend too much time practicing legato and proper articulation!

PURCELL
Minuet

This music was not written for the horn, but you must try to play it with the correct feeling, nevertheless. It is very stately, and must be performed with great dignity. Be sure to articulate clearly, and give each note its correct value. The third beat of measure 6 must not sound like a triplet figure. The piece is very short, so it is a good idea to make all the repeats.

ILYINSKY
Lullaby

This is another extremely legato piece. Play between the notes, follow the curve, and make a musical line. You will need to have an unremitting flow of air!

The grace notes, which occur first at number 11, must be very clear. I believe the best way to play them is to make a slight diminuendo before them, without losing the flow of air.

COHEN
Legend of the Hills

There are many possibilities for expression in this piece. If you make a slight diminuendo on the dotted half notes in measures 6 and 8, you will be better able to articulate the triads which follow.

You will need another style of articulation in the *poco animato* section. What you should aim for is a compromise between legato and staccato. This would be better than a dry staccato or a long legato.

After letter D, when it becomes forte, you must practice with the same kind of breath control that you use in piano passages. A common fault heard in loud horn passages is that the air column is not controlled, and the playing becomes wild and undisciplined. In loud playing, you must have as much or more control of the breath.

POOLE
Song of a City

Reid Poole has given us a fine bit of Americana, reminiscent of George Gershwin's "American in Paris." The composer supplied the following helpful performance notes:

"The opening portion, to letter B, should be played in expressive, legato, ballad style, with a full beautiful, tone. The section from B to D suggests the hustle and bustle of the city and calls for aggressive accents and staccato. Letter D returns to the songlike style. Always play with an affirmative full sound. Not too fast."

Listen carefully to the piano part at letter B, in order to get the *con moto* tempo. In measure 22, the fortissimo must be played full out, with the articulation riding on top of the air column. You must not stop the impetus of the musical line with your tongue. Be sure to play the lyrical section beginning in measure 25 with smooth legato, for contrast.

Myron Bloom

CONTENTS

CHORALE PRELUDE
"Herzlich tut mich verlangen"

♩ = 46 (1'43")

J. S. BACH

3 beats precede music

Adagio

8042

SERENATA

PIETRO BALLATORE

LITTLE RONDO

After Beethoven's Rondo in G for piano and violin

LUDWIG VAN BEETHOVEN

8042

ANDANTINO

♩ = 66 (2'23")

FRANZ SCHUBERT

4 beats precede music
Andantino

4 beats

ALLERSEELEN

♩ = 69 (2'52")

RICHARD STRAUSS, Op. 10, No. 8

8042

KAMARINSKAYA

P. TCHAIKOVSKY

8042

SOLILOQUY

DAVID KAPLAN

MINUET

♩ = 92 (1'07")

HENRY PURCELL

8042

LULLABY

♩ = 92 (1'50")

ALEXANDER ILYINSKY

8042

LEGEND OF THE HILLS

SOL B. COHEN

8042

SONG OF A CITY

REID POOLE

8042